A Witch's Grymoire of Secret Magick and Spells

by Gilly Sergiev

BARRON'S

This book is dedicated to my family of Weybourne Witches and to
the Goddess in every one of us because only when we recognize
who we truly are can we understand the power that we hold within.

First edition for North America published by Barron's Educational Series, Inc., 2002.

First published in 2002 under the title Witch's Box of Magick by Godsfield Press,
Laurel House, Station Approach, Alresford, Hants SO24 9JH, England

Text copyright © Gilly Sergiev
Package © Godsfield Press

Illustrations by Andrew Farmer

The right of Gilly Sergiev to be identified as the author of this work has been asserted
by her in accordance with the UK Copyright, Designs and Patents Act 1988.

All inquiries should be addressed to:
Barron's Educational Series, Inc.
250 Wireless Boulevard
Hauppauge, New York 11788
http://www.barronseduc.com

International Standard Book No. 0-7641-7533-5

Library of Congress Catalog Card No. 2001094435

Printed in China

9 8 7 6 5 4 3 2 1

Contents

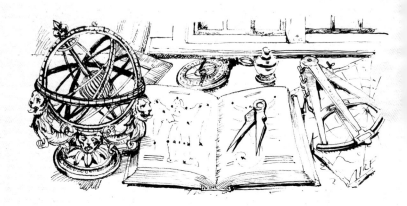

Creation

Witches' Lineage and Hierarchy

This is a book that only the brave will seek out and only the true of heart will understand, for I should not have needed to set pen to paper save for these sudden-changing and uncertain times. For this is the Grymoire of ancient magickal secrets that have long been known, passed down in spoken word alone, from daughter to daughter. Now I find I must write of this ancient knowledge to ensure the

survival of the Craft Lore— to keep safe these secrets for those who would know of them and wish to learn more. Many moons have passed since I danced as the Maid and healed as the Mother, and the Crone draws ever closer, beckoning me toward the delightful peace that is Summerland. The Wheel turns full circle, but to whom I write and how they will find this Grymoire, only the Goddess knows.

Holda, Hexen, Witches. We are all descended from the Goddess. We are her daughters and have all inherited her powers. How and where we choose to use our magick is between ourselves and the Great Mother. Witches are part of an unending ethereal family that is known about in secret and only among those who belong, and yet is open to all who seek. We have many names and yet none are needed, for we are all of the same family. This, then, is how it is. . .

Witches' Creation

*A*t the beginning there was only the Silent One: Sige. She had endured ceaselessly, wrapped in her heavy cloak of quiet and darkness; alone and yet not alone, great in her obmutescence. And in that time she thought of wondrous things, and the heights and depths of her thoughts were of stranger substance than we will ever know. The thoughts filled her spirit to such capacity that at last the moment came when she could be silent no longer. Roaming the Void, looking for a place to relive her thoughts and bring them to life, she finally found the Null.

And it was there that she was able to bring forth those thoughts that she had contained for so long: thoughts of the ether, the heavens, skies, and stars; the sun, moon, and seas; the earth and the Underworld. In her greatness, she brought forth all that is the macrocosm and the microcosm. And when she had done all this, she brought forth The First—her Daughter—the moon goddess Triformis, who ruled the waters, the earth, and the Underworld. Maid, Mother, and Crone. Venus, Gaia, and Hecate. In all that she was, Triformis was three. Immediately, thereafter, Triformis brought forth The

Second—the Sun God Actaeon—
who loved her. And in all that
he was, the Sun God was two.
And together they began to
spin the Great Wheel and
set the earth's cycle in motion.
And from that moment sprung
forth the Nature and her seasons. So the Wheel
gathered force and continued to spin, and the Silent One
returned back to her cloak of darkness and watched all
that was unfolding.

And while the Great Wheel spun and Sige
watched, a time came when the Sun God
Actaeon became two: the Oak King, son of
the goddess Triformis, and the Holly King,
consort of the goddess Triformis;
twin emanations of the Sun God
Actaeon. In the beginning, he was
born to Triformis as her son. He
grew to become the Oak King
Actaeon, who reigned supreme, deity of
the Waxing Wheel, until the time of the
summer solstice, when the Wheel began to

the oak of
the King

wane and the Holly King Actaeon arose to claim his crown.

At this time a great battle was fought between the two and the Oak King was slain.

And so now it was that the Holly King reigned supreme, deity of the waning Wheel. The Holly King reigned and loved the goddess Triformis as her consort, until again the Wheel spun and the time of the winter solstice arrived. The Oak King, reborn now, ordered the sacrifice of the Holly King. And so yet once more it happened that the Oak King reigned, waiting for his time of the summer solstice. And Triformis mourned for her consort, the Holly King, but walked the land with her son, the Oak King, knowing that the Wheel would ever spin thus.

And, thereafter, so it continued ad infinitum—the Wheel turning. First the Oak King of the waxing Wheel, then the Holly King of the waning Wheel, forever bound in a circle that is life, death, and rebirth. And while Actaeon remained above, he was known by all as the Great Sun God. But when he chose to walk the earth he became known as the Horned One, reflecting the celebration of his physical form of King Stag. And in this way Triformis found her balanced soul mate, Actaeon.

She was the Maid Venus Ana Isis, ruling the waters, 15 years of age and covered with apple blossom; the white new moon celebrating life and love with the King Stag. She was the Mother Gaia Babd Hathor, ruling the ground, 30 years of age and wreathed in roses; the red full moon celebrating birth and rebirth with her son, the Oak King. She was the Crone Hecate Macha Nephthys, ruling the Underworld, 60 years of age and carrying her basket of apples; the black dark moon celebrating sacrifice and death with the Holly King.

Sige watched all this and saw it was as it should be with life, death, and rebirth gathering force in everything it touched; and so, creation began.

King Stag

The ethereal family and its powers

Sige
The Silent One
Feminine Principal
Great Mother Goddess

Triformis
Triple Moon Goddess
Sea Maid Venus
Earth Mother Gaia
Underworld Crone
Hecate
Moon Queen (mother)

Maid   Mother   Crone

The four elements
Earth/North, Air/East,
Fire/South, Water/West:
corresponding to the four
corners of the Universe and
the four Great Winds

Actaeon
Sun God
Horned God, Cernunnos

The Stag King, Dyonnysis
Holly King (consort)/Oak King (son)
Sun King (father)/Star Lord (son)
Green Man
Corn King

Fire   Air

Earth   Water

Lords of the Watchtowers (elementals)

The cosmic cross comprising
North/Taurus, East/Aquarius,
South/Leo, West/Scorpio

Primal androgyne

Both sexes in one body
Right side male animal
power/left side female
Goddess magick.

The twins:

Adam+Lillith, Seth+Zoe,
Shiva+Kali, Amun+Hathor,
Hermes+Aphrodite,
Christ+Sophia
Anima and animus
Anima: female soul an—
heavenly ma—mother power.
Animus: male soul an—
heavenly mus—animal power

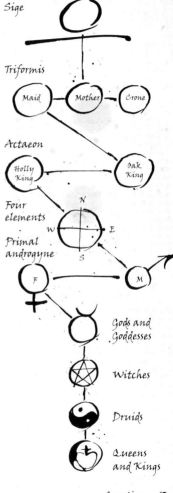

Sige

Triformis
Maid Mother Crone

Actaeon
Holly King   Oak King

Four elements

Primal androgyne

F   M

Gods and Goddesses

Witches

Druids

Queens and Kings

Gods, goddesses, and governing powers

Gods and goddesses of an infinite number, but including:

Three Graces who attend the Goddess:
Aglaia Agapeta (radiant truth), Thalia Theonia
(flowering unity), Euphrosyne Irene (joy of wisdom).

Three Furies who punish violation against
the Goddess: Alecto (the Endless; she who may not be
named), Tisiphone (the Retaliator; destruction), Megaera
(the Envious Ranger; grudge).

Three Fates who govern one's lot in life: Clotho Scribunda
(spinner of written destiny), Lachesis Ananka (weaver
of chance and what must be), Atropos Morgana (cuts the
thread of life; death).

Nine Muses attend the Goddess: Thalia (music),
Polyhymnia (sacred songs), Euterpe (flute
accompaniment), Clio (history), Calliope (heroic poetry),
Erato (erotic poetry), Terpsichore (dance), Melpomene
(tragedy), and Urania (celestial stars).

<u>Lud, King of the Upperworld, with the seven</u>
<u>Upperworld midwife emanations of Aquarius:</u>

i. Akki (humility)—midwife to the Aerial level,
   whose talisman is an agate with a snake
   engraved upon it

ii. Acco (kindness)—midwife to the Ethereal level,
   whose talisman is an emerald with a yoni
   engraved upon it

the yoni

iii. Akna (compassion)—midwife to the Olympial
   level, whose talisman is a sapphire with two
   entwined snakes engraved upon it

the snakes
entwined

iv. Acca (honor)—midwife to the Pyric level,
   whose talisman is a ruby with a snake engraved
   upon it

v. Ana (respect)—midwife to the Star level, whose
   talisman is a diamond with a dragon engraved
   upon it

vi. Acat (truth)—midwife to the Crystaline level,
   whose talisman is a crystal with a circle
   engraved upon it

vii. Zoe (love)—midwife to the Empyrean level,
   whose talisman is an onyx with a curled-up
   snake engraved upon it

the curled snake

<u>Hel, Queen of the Underworld, with the seven</u>
<u>Underworld porter emanations of Scorpio:</u>

i. Acru (arrogance)—porter to the Abyss level,
   whose amulet is gold with the head of a lion
   engraved upon it

ii. Agen (envy)—porter to the Chaos level, whose
    amulet is silver with a lingam engraved upon it

iii. Alphe (slander)—porter to the Anareta level,
     whose amulet is copper with a winged staff
     engraved upon it

the wingèd
staff

iv. Bun (deceit)—porter to the Purgatory level,
    whose amulet is iron with an eagle engraved
    upon it

v. Kham (sloth)—porter to the Hades level, whose
   amulet is fixed mercury with a sword engraved
   upon it

the crescent
moons

vi. Prince (lust)—porter to the Abbadon level,
    whose amulet is pewter with two crescent moons
    back to back engraved upon it

the sun

vii. Unu (greed)—porter to the Hel level, whose
     amulet is lead with the sun engraved upon it

the eye of
Horus

Other gods and goddesses,
and practitioners of magick:

Anathe: Warrior goddess who uses the death curse—
Anathema Maranatha. Angels: Archangels,
principalities, powers, virtues, dominions, thrones,
cherubim, and seraphim. Aruru and Aryaman: Makers
of humans from clay. Bards: Singers, poets, and history
makers. Chronos: God of time. Druidesses: Preservers of
magick, seers, prophetesses. Druids: Preservers of the
ancient tradition, priests, and teachers; interpreters of
omens and lore of tribe; representatives of the Stag King.
Fairies: "Little People of the Hills" with magickal powers,
descended from the Tuatha De Danann. Filid: Poets and
seers. Grimalkins: War witches who protect their own
using slander and a variety of negative powers such as the
"open look," the evil eye, the pointed finger, spoken or
written naming, objects empowered with curses, and
negative ritual magick inducing fear, such as "diabole,"
which is describing your enemy to the moon and asking for
retribution. Harpers: Music-makers. Hexen: Female
witches. Holda: Female witches. Kings: Human
descendants of Adam—power and arms. Lucina: Goddess

the sands
of time

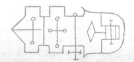

of witches.
<u>Menarva:</u>
Warrior
goddess of
wisdom and the
lunar calendar. <u>Nagna:</u>
Goddess of nudity.
<u>Nanshe:</u> Goddess of prophecy.
<u>Priestesses:</u> Preservers and initiators of religious rites.
<u>Queens:</u> Goddess descendants from the Otherworld—magick
and sorcery. <u>Satirists:</u> War witches using satire, loss of honor,
and violation of taboo as magick weapons against
wrongdoers. <u>Seers:</u> Visionaries; the ones who look into the
future. <u>Shamans:</u> Visitors to the Otherworld; prophets.
<u>Sorcerers:</u> Male witches. <u>Spirits and ghosts:</u> Visitors and
guests. <u>Tuatha De Danann:</u> Children of the Goddess Danu
(Mother of the Gods). <u>First pair of human twins:</u> Torn apart
from their primal androgyne status into two separate
beings—Adam and Lillith, Seth and Zoe.
<u>Vates:</u> Philosophers; interpreters of sacrifice.
<u>Witches:</u> Daughters and representatives of the Goddess,
keepers of nature, spellworkers in magick.
<u>Wizards:</u> Male witches.

Sabbats and Esbats

Sabbats and esbats are sacred times during the Wheel's year which pertain to the birth, death, and rebirth, and all corresponding movements of the Otherworld. Sabbats are held on the evening and following day of each sacred time, and concern particular movements of the ground. They are equidistant in the Wheel, falling every third month: February, May, August, and November. Esbats fall on the 21st day and are also equidistant in the Wheel, falling every third month: March, June, September, and December. They are the solstices and equinoxes, and concern particular movements of the sky. (Esbats are also used to describe any witch's meeting, be it weekly or monthly, where the daily Craft business is discussed.) Each sabbat has its relevant corresponding esbat that keeps the Wheel turning, starting with:

Yule Esbat (Winter Solstice)

December 21, all day —a time of rebirth

The Goddess gives birth to her son and all celebrate the new year and the new life. This is the shortest day of the year, with less sunlight than any other day, showing the Holly King's sacrifice by order of the new Oak King. Fires are lit to encourage the growth of the new sun god and new life. This is known in old as the Rose or Elder Meeting.

Rebirth, life, and rejuvenation: Yule/Oimelc/Ostara
Magick, fertility, and conception: Cetshamain/Litha/Bron Trogan
Rest, death, and into rebirth again: Mabon/Samhain/Yule

Oimelc (Imbolg) Sabbat

Midday on February 1 to midday on February 2—the ending of winter and the coming of milk to pasture

The Goddess in the form of Maid Brigantia, having given birth, is now rejuvenating, and the whole world follows suit. This is a time for celebrating the lushness of life, and ripeness is the roaming essence. This is known in old as the Birch or Rowan Meeting.

Ostara Esbat
(Spring Equinox)
March 21, all day—a time of reproduction

This is a celebration of new life and new awakenings with the Solar Wheel. The Wheel's hub

represents the sun, the spokes represent its rays, and the rim represents the surrounding nimbus. When the Solar Wheel is displayed on the altar, it represents the sun god come down to Earth to make fertile all that is lush. The Wheel is also thrown into water, representing the sun floating on the surface, symbolically fertilizing the water which, in turn, impregnates the crops. This is known in old as the Ash or Alder Meeting.

Cetshamain (Bel-tene) Sabbat
Midday on May 1 to midday on May 2 —the beginning of summer and the go-between of two fires

The Goddess unites in love with her consort (the god in the form of Belenos). Now fire purifies, and bonfires are lit to provide gateways through which we all pass into purification and strength. Sexuality and fertility are the roaming essences. Known in old as the Willow Meeting.

Lithe Esbat (Summer Solstice)

June 21, all day—a time of fertility

This is a celebration of love and sexuality. The sun is now at its maximum power, but the Holly King has arisen to claim his crown, killing the Oak King and taking his place, becoming the official consort of the Goddess. This is known in old as the Hawthorn or Oak Meeting.

Bron Trogan (Lughnassadh)

Midday on August 1 to midday on August 2—honor, feasting, and harvest

The Goddess, in her form of Mother Carmain, conceives, and so does the world. This is a time for visiting sacred sites.

Celebration marking the bringing in of

crops and a bountiful harvest is the roaming essence. This is known in old as the Holly Meeting.

Mabon Esbat (Autumn Equinox)
September 21 all day—a time of resting

The world is pregnant with possibilities, and all are waiting, conserving energy, and growing life within. This is known in old as the Hazel Meeting.

Samhain (Soween) Sabbat
Midday on October 31 to midday on November 1 —the opening of the Otherworld doors

The Goddess, in her form of Crone Morrigan, celebrates and yet mourns the passing of her consort into the Otherworld. This is the end of one year and the beginning of the next—a good time for making rituals and magicks and for scrying, and a special time for welcoming guests from the Otherworld. Spirituality is the roaming essence. This is known in old as the Vine or Ivy Meeting.

St. Michael's Mount

Glastonbury

Magickal Places

*T*he whole world itself is one magickal place. In days long
gone by, particular areas around the world signified
points on the cosmic map to aid those of mystical and
Otherworld abilities.

Ley lines—unseen but exact ethereal "roads"—run across
countries, joining mystical sites of pagan importance.
Magickal earth energies connect across the land in these
lines, which have points of access at the ancient sites along
them. Britain has many ley lines: from Glastonbury
through Stonehenge and on to Canterbury; from Cornwall's
St. Michael's Mount through Glastonbury and on to

The West Kennet Avenue, Avebury, Wiltshire

Avebury

Newgrange, Ireland

Avebury—all sites of great significance to witches.

Natural crossroads were another type of sacred place for witches to meet, being the symbolic joining point of the four corners of the world—North, East, South, and West—reflected in miniature on Earth. Sacred water areas, such as wells, springs, lakes, and marshes, opened certain doors to the Otherworld. Some mountainous areas in particular have been worshiped as gateways to the Otherworld, where rituals and rites were performed by the knowing few.

Wherever you live, you can be sure that you will find an ancient sacred site, whether it be water, mountain, ley line (pasture), or even volcano. The churches of yesteryear were often built over ancient pagan sacred sites, and can be thought of as excellent monuments to another secret time. Some sites, such as Stonehenge or Glastonbury Tor, have a power that is visible and obvious, but there are many less obvious sites. Whether you look into the depths of the Dead Sea or deep within Egypt's desert lands, there is a multitude of sites that strike a chord.

Stonehenge

Glastonbury

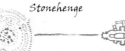

Canterbury

The Zodiac

Astrology and astronomy must join together if they are to see the whole picture, for they complement each other and are different facets of the same. They are the positive and negative energies, Ida and Pingala (see Chakras, page 55). Horoscopes, and in particular the individual aspects of the 12 known zodiac signs, cover a wide range of world-wide beliefs, from ancient magickal and pagan explanations to modern-day theories. The word "zodiac" comes from Greek—it means "circus of animals," which explains in brief the mystical circle within and without which lie the planets and stars corresponding to the horoscope. The word horoscope comes from the Greek word horoskopos, meaning "one who observes the hour."

The magickal explanation of the signs of the zodiac is this: Sige transformed herself into the snake goddess Aditi, then set Aditi free as a separate entity for the very purpose of creating her children—the signs of the zodiac. Forever after, in this shape, she was to be known as the Mother of the Zodiac. Every month for one lunar year, the goddess Aditi brought forth a child, and then in the thirteenth month she made her secret child who is yet to come. Twelve of her

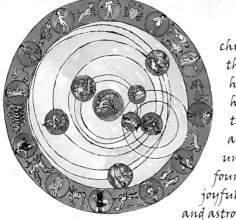

children are known but the thirteenth child is hidden, for that child holds many answers to the secrets of magick and is one by itself. This unknown child can be found only with the joyful union of astrology and astronomy. The 12 known signs have variously been represented by the 12 tribes of Israel, the 12 types of personality that make up mankind (representative of particular days), or the 12 disciples, metals, numbers, and so on.

The duality of the zodiac

Each one of the zodiac children has dual sexuality, with a corresponding twin, a yin and yang element, and a ruling ability reflected in mankind. In short and modern terms, the twins are known as they appear on the next page. If you add the numerical value of each twin's month together, you will see that it secretly points to and equals the number 13—the month of the esoteric lunar twin.

The Twins—old magick definitions

In old magick, the zodiac signs were known as follows:

Female Aquarius born in January and male Capricorn
        born in December—the 1st and 12th month
Female Pisces born in February and male Sagittarius
        born in November—the 2nd and 11th month
Male Aries born in March and male Scorpio
        born in October—the 3rd and 10th month
Female Taurus born in April and male Libra
        born in September—the 4th and 9th month
Female Gemini born in May and female Virgo
        born in August—the 5th and 8th month
Female Cancer born in June and male Leo
        born in July—the 6th and 7th month

<u>Taurus the Cow</u> was also known as Joseph;
also Friday, Copper, Venus, Dark Green,
Emerald, Simon Zelotes, and particularly
the yin and yang elements known in magick
circles as Bagdal and Araziel. Her ruling
abilities are ideas, integration, and action,
and she is responsible for health matters connected to the
throat and the neck. Taurus is also depicted on the cosmic
cross as one of the four ruling elementals, in the form of a
cow, and encompassing spring, Earth, and North. The
important Taurus element is depicted in the body of the
Great Sphinx. Her twin is Libra.

<u>Gemini the Two</u> was also known as Benjamin; also
Wednesday, Glass, Mercury, Yellow,
Diamond, James the Lesser, and
particularly the yin and yang
elements known in magick circles
as Sagras and Saraiel. Her ruling
abilities are vitality and
animation, and she is responsible for
health matters connected to the
shoulders and arms. Her twin is Virgo.

Cancer the Moon Child was also known as Reuben; also Monday, Silver, Moon, Pearl, Andrew, and particularly the yin and yang elements known in magick circles as Rahdar and Phakeil. Her ruling abilities are expansion and linking with spiritual guides, and she is responsible for health matters connected to the breasts and stomach. Her twin is Leo.

Leo the Lion was also known as Simeon; also Sunday, Gold, Sun, Amber, John, and particularly the yin and yang elements known in magick circles as Sagham and Seratiel. His ruling abilities are assurance and strength, and he is responsible for health matters connected to the back and the heart. Leo is also depicted on the cosmic cross as one of the four ruling elementals, in lion form, encompassing summer, Fire, and South. The important Leo element is depicted in the tail and feet of the great Sphinx. His twin is Cancer.

Libra the Justice was also known as Judah; also Friday, Copper, Venus, Seagreen, Turquoise, Bartholomew, and particularly the yin and yang elements known in magick circles as Grasgarben and Hadakiel. His ruling abilities are equilibrium and peacemaking, and he is responsible for health matters connected to the kidneys and loins. His twin is Taurus.

Virgo the Virgin was also known as Levi; also Wednesday, Glass, Mercury, Light Green, Jade, Philip, and particularly the yin and yang elements known in magick circles as Iadara and Schaltiel. Her ruling abilities are assimilation and spiritual adaptation, and she is responsible for health matters connected to the intestines and solar plexus. Her twin is Gemini.

<u>Scorpio the Scorpion</u> with Eagle Wings was also known as Dan; also Tuesday, Iron, Mars, Orange, Fire Opal, Thomas, and particularly the yin and yang elements known in magick circles as Riehol and Saissaiel. His ruling abilities are creativity and fertility, and he is responsible for health matters connected to the sex organs and bowels. Scorpio is also depicted on the cosmic cross as one of the four ruling elementals, in eagle form, encompassing Fall, Water, and West. The important Scorpio element is depicted in the eagle wings of the Great Sphinx. His twin is Aries.

<u>Sagittarius the Archer</u> was also known as Naphtali; also Thursday, Tin, Jupiter, Sapphire, James, and particularly the yin and yang elements known in magick circles as Vhnori and Saritaiel. His ruling ability is administration, and he is responsible for health matters connected to the hips and ovaries. His twin is Pisces.

Capricorn the Goat was also known as Gad; also Saturday, Lead, Saturn, Blue-black, Onyx, Matthew, and particularly the yin and yang elements known in magick circles as Sagdalon and Semakiel. His ruling abilities are discrimination and the absorption of negativity, and he is responsible for health matters connected to the knees and calves. His twin is Aquarius.

Aquarius the Midwife was also known as Asher; also Saturday, Lead, Saturn, Uranus, Violet, Aquamarine, Amethyst, Thaddeus-Jude, and particularly the yin and yang elements known in magick circles as Archer and Ssakmakiel. Her ruling ability is psychic intuition, and she is responsible for health matters connected to the ankles and circulation. Aquarius is also depicted on the cosmic cross as one of the four ruling elementals, in human form, encompassing winter, Water, and West. The important Aquarius element is depicted in the human face of the Great Sphinx. Her twin is Capricorn.

Aries the Ram was also known as Zebulon; also Tuesday, Iron, Mars, Red, Ruby, Peter, and particularly the yin and yang elements known in magick circles as Sataaran and Sarahiel. His ruling ability is aspirational prosperity, and he is responsible for health matters connected to the head and face. His twin is Scorpio.

Pisces the Fishes was also known as Issacher; also Thursday, Tin, Jupiter, Neptune, Turquoise, Aquamarine, Judas Iscariot, and particularly the yin and yang elements known in magick circles as Rasamasa and Vacabiel. Her ruling ability is visionary dreaming, and she is responsible for health matters connected to the feet and nails. Her twin is Sagittarius.

Tarot

Despite the prolific and conflicting information that abounds about where the tarot first originated, whether it be from ancient Egypt, Atlantis, India, Italy, France, or the Gnostics, the fact remains that it is one of our most important esoteric clues to the meaning of life. It doesn't actually matter where the tarot originated because the

T = Theory
A = Adaptation
R = Realization
O = Objectivity
T = Truth

important fact to hold on to is that it does survive, and if one can penetrate its esoteric meanings, one has a guide to follow and advice to consume in order to become that most wonderful of things: a whole person.

The original tarot was thought to contain 86 cards, but through the ages eight cards disappeared, thought by some to be Faith, Hope, Charity, The Papess, Earth, Air, Fire, and Water. Today's 78-card deck

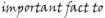

The Moon

The Hermit

comprises 56 Suit Cards (the Minor Arcana—Lesser Secrets) and 22 Trump cards (the Major Arcana—Greater Secrets).

The four suits of the cards are Pentacles (or Coins), relating to Earth, security, and money; Discs (or Cups), relating to Water, love, and emotions; Swords (or Epées), relating to Fire, action, and strength; and Staves (or Wands), relating to Air, conflict, and success. Some people prefer Swords to relate to Air, and Wands to relate to Fire—there is some disagreement over these two meanings. It is for you to decide which seems more appropriate.

Tarot is essentially akin to the mystic's occult Tree of Life: the Qabala—the Essence of Human Alchemy, or the Jewish mysticism of Kabbalah ("received doctrine"). It is a mass of secret and otherworldly information, and each person who delves into it will be individually rewarded in quite different ways. For something so important, it would be impossible to condense the information into a few paragraphs, so I will give you my overview of what the tarot is about and why it would be very empowering for all of us to study it.

In a simple form, the tarot is a collection of pictured and numbered cards that relate to an heroic journey through life, with the 0 card, The Fool, representing the traveler hero. The Fool, usually a male character with an animal such as a dog or a crocodile attacking at the feet, is representative of "the innocent" rather than the idiotic—the foolishness of one's nature implying the naïveté of a person who has not yet learned anything. At the start of the tarot's journey we are all naïve, and so we are all cosmically fools.

The end card is the number 21, relating to The World, and this usually depicts a female character dancing in joy. The Fool has transformed during the tarot's journey into an all-understanding and enlightened feminine being. Along the journey, the cards numbered 1 to 21 show unlimited ways of accessing knowledge about life, about oneself, and about others. There is no end to their information—how much is read into the cards and taken from them is up to the individual traveler. There are literally hundreds of ways of reading the cards and identifying with them.

A good way to begin to get acquainted with the cards is to lay them out with The Fool at the top followed by three exact rows of seven cards each: 1 to 7, 8 to 14, and 15 to 21, one row above the other. In this type of spread you can immediately see the whole of the life's journey, and how specific points relate to others. Use the tarot for divination and spiritual growth and the answers will all be revealed. I believe that the ultimate purpose of the tarot's guidance to us is that, in order to be complete, we must all find the feminine power within (the Goddess), which transforms the questions of life we all struggle with into the certain knowledge and wonder of the truth.

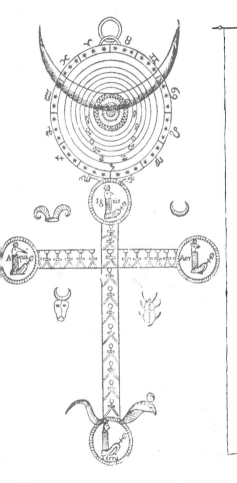

The Ether

This is magickal energy, also known as prana or chi, which is around us, inside us and outside us, above us and below us, within all things and without all things. It is constantly moving and changing its physical components, and by connecting with it, we too can change our physical components. Spells are moved by the power of the ether. It is the ultimate life force of the Goddess in all her glory.

Mysteries
Flying

*I*n days of yore, the first essential tool for flying was the
secret mixture of hallucinogenic herbs that re-created the
experience of flight. These were extremely dangerous herbs,
such as aconite, thornapple, henbane, fly agaric fungus,
and deadly nightshade, which were mixed with shortening
and applied to the skin. In these enlightened days, one
cannot possibly encourage the use of dangerous and illicit
drugs, no matter how "natural" they appear to be. The
above drugs can kill, and anyone experimenting with them
is asking for trouble. So don't use them. Be wiser. Simple

alternatives that are not harmful can be found, which stimulate the senses connected with the sensory experience of flying. For example, peppermint or cucumber when rubbed on the feet gives a cool and tingling sensation; a glass of red wine can stimulate; and so on. Therefore, depending on how deep your level of concentration and meditation is, you can experience the sensory effects of flying by using safe alternative herbs while you carry out magick.

The second important tool for flying was the broomstick, upon which one sat, lay, or curled up before starting the magick. The third important tool was the particular Mana and Numen used—the types of moon spirit magick and revelation that a witch called upon to facilitate her workings. These magicks included breathing techniques, vibrations, sounds, visualization, and invocations. Essentially, with a combination of the three important tools, the witch would enter a deep meditational level, and to all intents and purposes, her etheric double would leave her body and fly to wherever she or he wished to go.

Scrying

*T*he term scry—"to use the divining crystal"—comes from the word descry, which means "succeed in discerning," which in turn means "gain insight." It is not just the divining crystal that is used, but any polished or reflective surface, such as black stone, water, oil, mirrors, and so on. Reading the tarot, runes, or palmistry could also be seen as scrying, simply from the fact that you are gaining insight. However, in witches' terms, to scry usually means to look into the crystal ball or another reflective surface in order to discern something.

The crystal ball traditionally should be used only after midday, and ideally only at nighttime. It is a tool of the moon, and therefore should have only the moon's rays upon it. Any sun ray would damage it, and a detailed cleansing and ritual washing would need to be done to reinstate its moon magick. Keep your crystal or mirror under a black cloth to absorb harmful daylight energy, and always use it in a darkened room by the light of a candle. An incense favorable for scrying is myrrh, although every scent has a different connotation. Look for a scent attuned to the Otherworld and mystic ability.

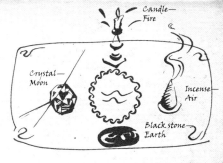

Crystals and mirrors should be washed in a solution of vinegar and spring water and rubbed with a dry, clean cloth. Sprinkling spring water over a crystal not only enlarges certain images within the crystal and brings particular points to your notice, but also connects with the Water elemental. A candle is symbolic of the Fire elemental; incense of the Air elemental; a magick stone nearby—or the wooden table or floor that the crystal stands on—of the Earth elemental; and the crystal itself of the spirit. So before you even start scrying, you are guarded and guided by the spiritual energy around you.

Everyone has a different way to scry and a different time band to tune in to, so it is not usual to tune in as soon as you gaze within the depths. Prayers and rituals and soft or subliminal music help. The essence is to lose yourself from this world and gain access to that world. Because of the power of the crystal resonance or the mirror's atoms, you will find this comes easily. Relax and focus on the Otherworld by not concentrating at all. Drift and let the images, thoughts, and words come to you. It is for you to find your own way.

Banishing

*T*he function of banishing is to get rid of an unwanted spiritual energy. Whenever you feel the presence of an unwanted entity from the spirit world, cast a magick circle with your wand and summon the power of thought. Then, facing each of the four compass points in turn, make the sign of the pentacle with your wand, saying: "I call upon the Goddess Triformis, Maid, Mother, and Crone; and with the same power of the One, I banish all negative and senseless thoughts, words, and deeds directed at this person.

"I send the power of the pentacle to dissolve their negative energy and bring light where there was dark, and free this child of the Goddess. All negative energy aimed at me, I return to the sender, three times three. Amen."

Point to remember
If you are male, always move in the direction of the sun: deosil (clockwise).
If you are female, always move in the direction of the moon: widdershins (counterclockwise).

The Righteous Sword of Fire

*U*sing the imagery of the Righteous Sword of Fire is another very effective way of conducting a banishing. Stand facing South, then relax and imagine yourself holding a large, shining, golden sword in your right hand. Now imagine yourself growing taller and stronger, clothed in armor and golden fire, as you become a warrior of the magickal realms.

Now say:

> "In the name of Hecate I take
>   up the Sword of Righteous Fire
> For my defense against all evil
>   in the Righteous Fight."

Beginning at the South, draw a circle with the sword (widdershins for female witches), pointing at the floor and imagining the circle of flames streaming from the sword's tip, glowing with white and golden light as you circle the area. When back at the South, hold the sword high with point upraised, and say:

"May the power of Hecate and the angels of the
world recognize the holder of the Righteous Sword
and guide me in all that I do.
Again I say, may the power of Hecate and the
angels of the world be at my side in the
Righteous Fight.
Once more I say, may the power of Hecate
and the angels of the world be with
me henceforth. Amen."

Lower your sword and with a mighty push
imagine sinking its blade into the earth.

Sealing the Aura, or the Qabalistic Cross Ritual

This ritual can be done at any time and will strengthen
your aura and protect you from any random
negativity. Stand facing North and seal the aura (make
the Qabalistic cross sign) on the body. Using your left hand,
and with the first two fingers pointing:

Touch your forehead and say, "To thee O Goddess...".
Touch your breast bone and say,
"...be the All Sacred Dominion...".
Touch your left shoulder and say,
"...and the All Blessed Glory...".
Touch your right shoulder and say,
"...of the All Divine Power...".
Clasp your hands together and say,
"...until the end of time and beyond.
In your gracious name. Amen."

Onions or garlic strewn around the house (see p. 91) will absorb any negativity—especially when you are unsure of people visiting you. Once the people have gone or the moment has passed, the onion or garlic is poisonous—so you must either burn it, bury it, or throw it in water to get rid of it. Wild thistles are also used in this way, and can be carried on the person as a charm to deflect negativity. They are said to guard against thieves in particular.

The Psychic Police

The psychic police[†] can be attracted into your life by drawing the sigil of a scarlet or red circle with a black solar cross in the middle (the solar cross is a well-known sigil for the key to the Otherworld). In essence, to call on the psychic police, you should meditate on the symbol while sending out a request for help.

I have adopted this custom and used it once at a particularly trying time in my life. While meditating on the sigils I had the intense feeling of a powerful protective force around me, although I physically saw nothing. Later that night as I slept, I had a wonderful dream. I dreamed that I was standing in a dark room with the negativity behind me. Suddenly, I began to rise effortlessly into the air, and as I looked up I saw before me the famous sigil of a triangle with an eye depicted inside it (the triangle is a magickal sigil in itself and the eye represents the mystic "third eye"). I floated toward the sigil and just before diving into it, I woke up! Bizarrely, some may say, my problems disappeared within one week.

[†] The psychic police are first introduced in Dion Fortune's book, Psychic Self Defence.

The psychic police are a body that you yourself should apply to and make your own decisions about, but I certainly believe in their protective qualities, whether their power is formed from witches and wizards secretly gathered together in this world or the other. My psychic police sigil now contains the triangle with the eye in it, because it is particularly relevant to me. However, now is not the time to talk of these things—they are in your tomorrow.

Familiars

A familiar is a witch's attendant, and a famulus is a wizard's or magician's attendant. They are mostly animal in form, but sacred-magick in spirit. Known most commonly these days under the one word "familiar," meaning "attendant," they serve the witch by using their unique powers. They can concentrate magickal energy in different ways, such as by hearing far-off events and informing the witch in advance, by aiding in healing practices, or by warning of negative energies.

The Cat: The moon, ancient secrets, communication, and travel

The Frog: Fertility and rain

Familiars usually speak in an individual language understood by the witch. A few of the more well-known familiars and their particular associations and strengths are listed below.

The Cow: The moon and fertility

The Horse: Epona, Diana, and travel

The Swan: Purity, good luck, and rebirth

The Bear: The moon and water

The Deer: Fertility and prosperity

The Fish: Wisdom and magickal power

The Bull: Fertility and protection

The Duck: Healing and sun power

The Crane: Sexuality and taboo

The Ram: Sexuality and strength

The Raven: The delivery of knowledge—a messenger

The Dog: The moon and the Underworld

The Snake: Fertility and rebirth

The Bat: Success and bringer of luck

The Hare: Moon power—faithful and self-sacrificing

The Goat: Magick and healing

The Owl: Wisdom of the moon

The Snail: Healing and moon power

The Wolf: The moon and heat

The Pentacle

The pentacle is a powerful and magickal sigil comprising a five-pointed star (pentagram) within a circular disc (pentacle). The power stems from its combination of potent sigils:

> Circle—Sige
> Star—Actaeon
> Five points—the
>   four elements plus
>   Triformis

All these elements comprise the Holy Family. The Egyptians used this figure as a hieroglyph for "womb in the earth," and a strong connection with witch-priestess ritual is evident. If the pentagram points upward, it is referring to life-giving energy (yang), and if it points downward, it is referring to death-giving energy (yin). The pentagram is also one of the better known formal positions that a witch stands in when spellcasting, using the raised cone of power: head raised (point one), two arms outstretched (points two and three), and two legs outstretched (points four and

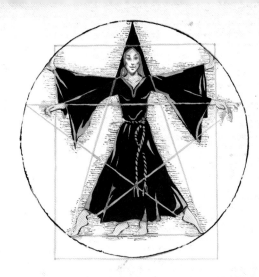

the body makes a
pentagram

five). One of the well-known ritual invocations of the
pentacle from around the time of the Abra-Melin (an
ancient Gnostic theory of magick) is:

Touch your third eye (between the eyebrows) and say,
    "Atoh..." (unto thee).

Touch your breast and say, "...malkus..." (the kingdom).

Touch your right shoulder and say, "...ve-gevurah..."
    (the power).

Touch your left shoulder and say, "...ve-gedulah..."
    (the glory).

Clasp your hands together and say, "...le-olahm. Amun."
    (forever. Amen.)

Sympathetic Magick

This is magick that is done in sympathy with the object or desire you wish to attain. By imitating something, you acquire that thing's essence and can then work with it. For example, when performing the Drawing Down the Moon ritual (see page 76), the witch-priestess is in sympathy with the Goddess and, by wearing her sigils and by ritual prayer, becomes Her in the magick ceremony. The druid-priest wears stag horns tied to his head and also sigils to symbolize and become the real Stag King. Poppets are another type of sympathetic magick, because the poppet "doll" is in sympathy with your image or another person's image, and then becomes alive through the symbolism. All types of sympathetic magick occur when the object or person literally takes on the appearance or essence of the thing it wishes to work with.

the druid-priest becomes the real Stag King—by the use of ceremonial antlers

Chakras

Spinning energy wheels of the cosmos are reflected in us in seven prime body centers known as chakras. The positive and negative energies that come from the chakras are known as Ida and Pingala. When they are balanced through deep and controlled meditation, they can transform the chakras into pure light. When all chakras are spinning at full light power, the witch is engulfed in a blazing and healing aura of light force, which enables the highest kinds of spellwork to be accomplished. The health of an individual is also at its peak, and the person experiences total well-being. However, if the chakras are out of sync with each other, they can be aligned with their corresponding colors and crystals, balancing and restoring the body's energy centers.

<u>The crown chakra</u> spins in and around the crown of the head and responds to the color variations of purple and the crystals amethyst, carnelian, diamond, and rhodonite; and the metal copper. In the body, the crown chakra is concerned with the central nervous system, the brain, spirituality and mental ability, nerves, sleep, and the pineal gland.

The third eye chakra spins in and around the middle brow and responds to the color variations of dark blue and the crystals agate, amazonite, moonstone, and peridot; and the metal bronze. In the body, the third eye chakra is concerned with the eyes, the pituitary gland, mental and emotional disorders, and the hypothalamus.

The throat chakra spins in and around the throat and responds to the color variations of light blue and the crystals howlite, azurite, blue sapphire, chrysocolla, and mother-of-pearl. In the body, the throat chakra is concerned with the respiratory system, the lymphatic system, creativity and memory, and the thyroid.

The heart chakra spins in and around the center breast and responds to the color variations of green and the crystals aventurine, ruby, sodalite, and emerald; and the metal gold. In the body, the heart chakra is concerned with the circulation, the immune system, blood pressure, love and compassion, and the thymus.

The solar plexus chakra spins around the center stomach and responds to the color variations of yellow and the crystals quartz, green jasper, obsidian, and jet. In the body, the solar plexus chakra is concerned with the stomach and digestion, stress and emotions, and the pancreas.

The sacral chakra spins around the navel and responds to the color variations of orange and the crystals dolomite, hematite, moonstone, bloodstone, and garnet; and the metal silver. In the body, the sacral chakra is concerned with fertility, the kidneys, the bladder, intuition, and the ovaries.

The base chakra spins around the base of the spine and responds to the color variations of red and the crystals carnelian, tiger's eye, kunzite, onyx, and yellow zircon. In the body, the base chakra is concerned with reproduction, survival, the ego, confidence, and the adrenals.

Rituals

Magick Circle and Cone of Power

S ome ancient traditions insist that a magick circle should be exactly 9 feet (2.7 m) in diameter, consisting of two outer rings with a pentacle in the middle making the third ring, and cast with an athame (ritual knife). This is certainly a beautiful and potent image of a magick circle, and one that I would advise using if it is within your power to lay it out so. However, in witchcraft a circle can be of any size and made of any substance. Any circle that you conjure and then make magick in will work. Within your circle, you raise your own cone of power.

The mere image of a circle is more powerful than many will ever know, and in witchcraft there are no exact rules to anything because we are all different and so, too, are our abilities. I personally use a wand to conjure my circle, because I am particularly suited to the Air dynamic and the East. So follow your instincts and witch feelings, and your circle will be the most powerful circle for you.

To aid you when first starting, a traditional way to conjure a magick circle is through the power of the elementals. When bathed and robed, and having fasted if deemed necessary, stand at your altar facing East, then take your wand and proceed to draw a magick circle around you and yours. Raise the sacred wand and slowly move in the direction of a circle, widdershins, to North, West, South, and back to East. Envision an enchanted white cloud of power flowing from your wand and creating a mystical circle as you move. This white cloud strengthens and grows to fully encompass you and yours from the highest to the deepest to the widest points, until you are standing fully within a magick circle.

From the central point you can now raise the cone of power, spiraling down into you or up out of you, from or toward the highest point. If you require power to aid your spellworking, kneel in front of the altar and raise your two arms wide and high so the power can funnel into you. If you require power to send your spellworking out into the ether, then kneel in front of the altar but lower your two arms downward to touch the ground so that the power is channeled into the earth. The cone of power will grow in strength as you chant, dance, and spellwork.

Give your mind over totally to this magick and you will be imbued with strength and lifeforce and able to help others as you so wish. When done with your spellwork, ring the bell three times, and after each ring say: "It is done." Now place both hands on your pentacle and stay for a few moments reflecting on your new-found powers. When you feel ready and calm, withdraw the magickal circle back into your wand by standing again at the East and pointing your wand while moving deosil— South, West, North, and back to East—and envisioning the white cloud rushing back into your wand.

Lords of the Watchtowers— Seal of the Pentacle

*B*efore the recognized religions of the world took hold and changed them, there were names and stories of magickal content well known by all. Over time, these names and stories became infused with other religious context, and a lot of their primordial magickal knowledge was lost. This is an original explanation of the Watchtower Lords, and may seem confusing alongside some of their later institutionalized images.

There are two male and two female Lords—the name "Lord" signifying a magickal status rather than a sexual one. Each Lord is situated at a corner of the world at the four points of the compass, corresponding to the elements. They are individually known as the four archangels, but in truth have names far older. Together they are known as the Tetrad and their symbol is the equidistant cross or the "cosmic cross." The Tetrad guides and protects your spiritual development and watches over the nations of the world. Calling on the Lords of the Watchtowers will protect and enlighten you in all that you do.

ㄹユㄣ升・タ⌒ム/ ∫ㄥㅠL

Lords of the Watchtowers

Cosmic
cross

At the North watchtower reigns
the mighty archangel Auriel.
She is the Lord of Earth and
her helpers are the Gnomes.
Her name is Nanta and her
color is green. Her symbol is the
sacred cow.

At the West reigns the mighty
archangel Gabriel. She is the Lord of Water, her
helpers are the Undines. Her name is H'coma, her color blue,
her symbol the sacred scorpion with eagle feathers.

At the South watchtower reigns the mighty archangel
Michael. He is the Lord of Fire and his helpers are the
Salamanders. His name is Bitom and his color is red.
His symbol is the sacred lion.

At the East watchtower reigns the mighty archangel
Raphael. He is the Lord of Air and his helpers are the
Sylphs. His name is Exarp and his color is white. His symbol
is the sacred human figure.

Earth

Air

Water

Sun

Lords of the Watchtowers ritual

Using your altar or a round table, inscribe the names of the four Lords and place an object to represent their force at the right place: a stone in the North for the Lord of Earth; a chalice in the West for the Lord of Water; a candle in the South for the Lord of Fire; burning incense in the East for the Lord of Air. Stand facing the North and raise your wand or athame. Then, while swaying gently, whisper softly to the North: "Watch over me, dearest Nanta Earth, and safeguard me from all evil nearing from the North. With a seal and power of the pentacle, I cast all evil directed at me back to the sender, three times three." Make the sign of the pentacle in the direction of North with your wand or athame, and envision any negativity rushing back to the sender with the triple force of three.

Now turn to the West and whisper again softly: "Watch over me, dearest H'coma Water, and safeguard me from all

evil nearing from the West. With a seal and power of
the pentacle, I cast all evil directed at me back to the
sender, three times three." Make the sign of the
pentacle in the direction of West, and envision
any negativity rushing back to the sender.

Now turn to the South and whisper softly: "Watch over
me, dearest Bitom Fire, and safeguard me from all evil
nearing from the South. With a seal and power of the
pentacle, I cast all evil directed at me back to the
sender, three times three." Make the sign of the
pentacle in the direction of South, and envision any
negativity rushing back to the sender.

Now turn to the East and whisper softly: "Watch over
me, dearest Exarp Air, and safeguard me from all evil
nearing from the East. With a seal and power of the
pentacle, I cast all evil directed at me back to the sender,
three times three." Make the sign of the pentacle in the
direction of East with your wand or athame, and
envision any negativity rushing back to the sender
with the triple force of three.

Finally, turn back to the North, then point your wand or
athame to the ground and say: "As I will it, in the sacred
name of the Tetrad, so will it be. Amen."

Initiation

*I*nitiation happens when a
person is ready and
happy to accept the
realities of becoming
a witch and all that
it entails. Initiation is
the time when either among
others in a coven, or as a singular by oneself, a ceremony is
enacted to confirm the new witch's identity to the
Otherworld and to this one by his or her sacred rebirth. It is a
time when a new name is given and received and
celebrations are made, officially welcoming the witch into
a new and wonderful family. Ceremonies vary, of course,
because of individuals' and coven members' histories, but
the overall theme is one of welcoming a new power to the
cosmic circle. Bread is eaten as the "partaking of the fruit of
the earth," wine is drunk as the "partaking of the spirit of
the one," and salt is consecrated in water as the "sacred
mysteries hidden in all things."

Consecration: the blessing of salt and water

Perform this ritual using your first two fingers. Point your fingers at the salt and say: "I exorcize thee, sacred essence of Earth, by the living Goddess, the Maid Venus; by the holy Goddess, the Mother Gaia; by the omnipotent Goddess, the Crone Hecate; that thou mayest be purified of all evil influences in the name of Actaeon, the sun god, Lord of Angels."

Point your fingers over the salt and say: "Sacred essence of Earth, exult in thy creation. In the name of Sige, the One, maker of all things, and of Actaeon, the sun god, I consecrate thee to the service of the goddess Triformis, in her absolute and righteous name. Amen."

Point your fingers at the water and say: "I exorcize thee, sacred essence of Water, by the living Goddess, the Maid Venus; by the holy Goddess, the Mother Gaia; by the omnipotent Goddess, the Crone Hecate; that thou mayest be purified from all influences in the name of Actaeon, the sun god, Lord of Angels."

Point your fingers over the water and say: "Sacred essence of Water, exult in thy creation. In the name of Sige, the One, maker of all things, and of Actaeon, the sun god, I consecrate thee to the service of the goddess Triformis, in her absolute and righteous name. Amen."

Now cast the salt into the water and say: "We pray to thee, O Goddess, Mother of the Waters, the Earth, and the Underworld. Love who is over all that is visible and invisible, we ask that thou embrace these creatures of the elements, cast forth thy powerful gaze, and bless them with thy Sacred name. Give to this salt the power that may make for health of body, and give to this water the power that may make for health of soul, so that there may be banished from this place where they are used every power of adversity and every illusion of evil, for the sake of Actaeon, the sun god, and in the name of the Goddess, the one true love and the light and the dark. Amen."

Water consecrated with salt may be used as a sacred bath, for creating circles, for making sacred sigils upon a person, or for sprinkling around a place.

Handfasting

The handfasting ritual is a celebration of twin souls meeting and becoming one by re-enacting their original status of primal androgyne and affirming their desire to be bound together as long as they wish, for all to see in this physical life and before the sacred love of the Goddess. It is the original pagan rendition of the later marriage ceremony. There is no tie to the length of time a handfasting lasts; it is beyond human rules and regulations. Handfasting is a wedding of the mystical and the human, and as such its ritual belongs to the laws of nature.

The coven or group meets in a sacred place of celebration, such as some

The traditional way, from 'The Arnolfini Marriage' by Jan van Eyck

wooded outdoor area where others cannot disturb the ceremony but where the whole of the ethereal world is gathered. Everyone dresses in their best finery and is wreathed with flowers and ribbons, as well as greenery, such as green broom, for good luck and a rich life. The two persons being handfasted should be dressed in white robes, symbolizing purity, the woman wearing a wreath of ivy and the man wearing a wreath of holly, symbolizing female and male joy. Each should wear a ring for love, silver in color for the woman and gold in color for the man, and a brooch over the breast area, symbolizing purity of heart. If it is possible, they should both carry a little rosemary, rue, and garlic for happiness and good fortune.

Before the start of the ceremony, the area to be used is sprinkled with blessed salt, then all participants sweep the area using their brooms to clear away any negative energy. Friends and coven members then join hands to form a circle around the boundaries of the area to be used. Once the circle is made, the hands are dropped and each member stays in place for the duration of the ritual. The two principal initiates stand in the circle, together with a priestess, druid, and bard. In the center of the circle is the altar, wreathed in flowers and white candles, with a cauldron of water in the middle. Directly in front of the altar on the ground lies the sacred broom of the priestess.

The bard plays upon the harp and drum and bell. He is the officiating musical member, calling up the elementals and pleasing all with his song. The druid quietly chants the spells of success and love and roams the circle, guarding the forces at work. He is the officiating spellworker, maintaining the power within the circle, overseeing the forces, and pleasing all with his magick. The druid represents the god element, although his primary function is to keep the forces of love and fortune spells woven while the ritual takes place. The priestess, who wears a red robe, calls the ceremony. She is the representative of the Goddess, joining the two in the handfasting ritual.

The friends and coven members in the circle around the sacred area lend their support, love, and magickal ability to the processes taking place. The magickal protection of the circle is made by the physical presence of the coven members and friends.

The Twitch

*T*he ceremony begins with everyone chanting The Twitch, softly at first, then rising to the loudest crescendo and stopping abruptly:

> "Blessed be, the power of three: priestess, druid, and bard. Twitch!
> Handfast new, the power of two: maid and man together. Twitch!
> Success is done, the power of one: love will rule this day. Twitch!
> As it will, so mote it be—twitch in all we do and see. TWITCH!"

The priestess then steps forward and takes the left hand of the woman and the right hand of the man and ties them loosely together with a white silken cord, saying: "By the power of the Arcadian, Isis [or Mary, or Ana] weaves her purity around these twin souls, binding them in this world as with a silken cord." The bard strikes one clear note upon the bell.

The priestess then ties a red silken cord around their two hands, saying: "By the power of the Mater Familias, Hathor [or Mary, or Babd] weaves her strength around these twin souls, binding them in this world as with a silken cord." The bard strikes a second clear note upon the bell.

The priestess then ties a black silken cord around their two hands, saying: "By the power of the Generatrix, Nephthys [or Mary, or Macha] weaves her wisdom around these twin souls, binding them in this world as with a silken cord." The bard strikes a third clear note upon the bell.

The priestess then turns to the woman and says: "[Name], do you come willingly to join with this man as his twin soul and to affirm the love of the Goddess?"

The woman says: "I come willingly to join with this man as his twin soul, and I affirm the love of the Goddess."

PRIESTESS: "I ask again: [Name], do you come willingly to join with this man?"

WOMAN: "I come willingly to join with this man."

PRIESTESS: "I ask once more: [Name], do you come willingly?"

WOMAN: "I do so come willingly."

The priestess takes up the cauldron and offers it to the woman, who drinks from it. Then the priestess replaces the cauldron on the altar. Next she turns to the man.

PRIESTESS: "[Name], do you come willingly to join with this woman as her twin soul, and to affirm the love of the Goddess?"

MAN: "I come willingly to join with this woman as her twin soul, and I affirm the love of the Goddess."

PRIESTESS: "[Name], I ask again, do you come willingly to join with this woman?"

MAN: "I come willingly to join with this woman."

PRIESTESS: "[Name], I ask once more, do you come willingly?"

MAN: "I do so come willingly."

The priestess takes up the cauldron again and offers it to the man, who drinks from it. She replaces the cauldron upon the altar, then drinks from it, followed by the druid and the bard. She then places her hands on top of the

couple's bound hands and says: "So mote it be. All here
so present do witness these rites: by the power of the primal
androgyne that Triformis has conferred on these twin souls,
let no attendant despoil. May this moment be noted in the
Halls of Akash and may these twin souls be joined unto
their time, blessed by the Mother and Father and three times
by all of all of all. So mote it be. Blessed be. Amen." All
present repeat: "Blessed be. Amen." The bard strikes
the bell three times.

The cords are unwound from the couple's hands, and the
priestess then takes her broom and lays it in front of the
couple. Holding hands, the couple runs and jumps over the
broom. Now the friends and coven members one by one
(unwinding the circle) approach the altar and dip their
hands in the water and then sprinkle it over their friends
as they give them a particular wish, initiating the start of
the handfasting celebrations. The celebrations take on the
particular desires of the couple, but usually will
include present-giving, eating, drinking,
singing, dancing, and music, well into the
early hours.

a broom for leaping o'er

Drawing Down the Moon

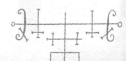

This ritual is usually performed on the night of a full moon, although it can be used at any other time when the power of the Goddess is particularly needed in spellworking. The basic aim of the magick is for the witch-priestess to draw on the occult and magnetic powers of the moon and guide them into her body to temporarily become the Goddess. When a successful ritual has been performed, the witch-priestess, who has now become the Goddess in human form, has the added magickal potency of the moon, the stars, and the constellations within her, which adds esoteric and ancient power to her spellworking. As the Goddess, the witch-priestess can perform only three spells at a time.

Drawing Down the Sun

The only true time for a druid-priest to perform the twinned rite of Drawing Down the Sun is at the time of the summer solstice when the sun is at its most powerful. This masculine rite draws down the strength and warrior aspect of life and death into the druid-priest from the sun. Therefore, this masculine rite can only truly be performed once a year, and

as such the magick of the druid—who
becomes the God—is used mostly in times of
war and in the context of honor, fair play,
and justice.

(Note. The ritual for Drawing Down the
Sun is practically the same as Drawing
Down the Moon except that the roles are reversed:
the druid is the central figure with the witch in
attendance. Where the masculine druid differences occur in
the sun ritual, they have been put in brackets next to the
feminine Drawing Down the Moon rituals.)

Nine (seven) days before the ritual

Keep to a vegetarian diet and meditate daily for the nine
days before the ritual on what you are attempting to do
and why you are doing it. (Remain chaste for the seven
days before the ritual, in order to build up sexual energy
and strengthen the mind.)

Purify and cleanse the body daily with rose oil and
myrtle water.

Select brand-new tools for the ritual. These are a hazel
(oak) wand with steel (bronze) tips at either end, a black-
handled knife—athame—and a silver or white (gold or

athame

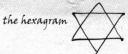

the hexagram

yellow) candle. Carry out spellwork over the tools and chant an incantation to animate them. Include in your chant the statement that it is your divine potential to stand as the earthly image of the Goddess (God), then ask for her (his) blessings and the power of the Watchers to guide you and to guard your work.

On the day of the ritual

Draw a circle within a circle on the floor in either chalk, salt, or flour. Draw a triangle in the middle of the two circles. Place around the inner circle band a pentagram, a hexagram, a small chalice of water, sandalwood incense, a charcoal brazier, and the power names Atanehndeged, Elion, Alpha, Omega, and Ideodamiach. These can be written either on pieces of paper or in salt, flour, or chalk. Have a bath in water scented with myrtle leaves and dress in a white flowing robe tied with a single white cord. Leave your hair unbound

bog myrtle

and your feet bare. You will need a small amount of consecrated oil (also called chrism) and a bell for this ritual. (Any oil can be consecrated by praying over it. Most witches make their own blend, adding balsam, honey, vanilla, or cloves to olive oil.)

When they are dressed and ready, the druid and the witch-priestess stand inside the circle. The witch-priestess (druid) stands inside the triangle, the druid (witch-priestess) stands just outside the triangle and facing her (him). To prepare herself, the witch breathes evenly and deeply and begins to chant "Amor, Amator, Amides" ("Amor, Plaior, Amator") over and over under her breath. While she does this, the group or coven move around the inner rim of the circle, clapping very softly and gently stamping the ground while they walk. The druid takes the consecrated oil and anoints the witch-priestess seven times: once on the third eye, quietly saying, "Power of the Moon, power of the Sun"; once on each shoulder, quietly saying, "Power of Mars, power of Saturn"; once on each breast, quietly saying, "Power of Sun (Moon), power of Venus"; and once on each wrist, quietly saying, "Power of Jupiter, power of Mercury." When the druid has finished anointing the witch, he now repeats a chant three times, which the group

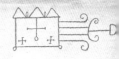

the druid
rings the
bell once

or coven repeat after him each time. As they do this, the clapping, stamping, and chanting rises in volume.

The druid says, "Abba, Abraxas, Elion" ("Escerchie, On, Adonai"), then rings a bell once. The witch-priestess raises her arms and says, "Omnipotent Lady, All Seeing Love, channel thy heavenly magick. I draw down thy moon power and unto me, we are one, thou art me, I am thee." ("Supreme Lord, Warrior King, Keeper of the Peace, channel thy holy magick. I draw down thy sun power and unto me, we are one, thou art me, I am thee.") The druid rings the bell once again.

The witch continues, "I that am all now stand before thee, my head reaches to the burning lights. I that am the nature of all things, my body embraces all that is warm. I that am the great silence borne on the wind, my toes touch the deep dark sleep. Behold Sige-Triformis, I am light, I am love, I am she. Agla Ata nehen deged. Amen." ("I that am ever now stand before thee, my head reaches to the burning lights. I that am the fire in all things, my body embraces all that is warm. I that am the great voice borne on the

wind, my toes touch the deep dark sleep. Behold Adonai-
Actaeon, I am light, I am love, I am he. Agla Ata nehen
deged. Amen.") The group or coven repeats "Amen" and the
druid rings the bell for the third time and says, "It is done."
All present shout, "It is done." The Goddess can now perform
a maximum of three spells within the magick circle and
with the druid and group aiding her.

Closing the ritual

Before closing the circle, and at the end of the ceremony, the
Goddess kneels inside the triangle with both hands pressed to
the ground. The circle moves back softly and quietly stamps
and claps in a widdershins movement around the perimeter
of the circle. The druid sprinkles holy water over the head of
the Goddess and says, "With good despatch, Lady of Heaven,
Most Blessed Goddess, and all that is love, until we meet
again in the flesh. Amen." ("With good despatch, Lord of
Hosts, Most Supreme God, and all that is high, until we
meet again in the flesh. Amen.") The druid then makes the
sign of the pentacle over the head of the Goddess and she
replies, "With good despatch until we meet again in the

flesh, I return this witch to her sacred form and to thee all present in the name of love. Amen." ("With good despatch until we meet again in the flesh, I return this druid to his sacred form and to thee all present in the name of peace. Amen.")

At this point an alternative form of the Lord's Prayer can be said for the Goddess ritual, which is the same except for the beginning, which starts, "Our Mother who art in Heaven…" (The God ritual would have the Lord's Prayer as standard, which starts, "Our Father who art in Heaven…") Now the circle is closed in the usual way of the group or coven and a celebration takes place.

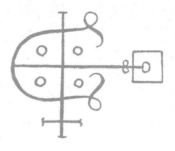

The Great Rite

The story of this ritual, also known as the Banais Rigi or Royal Marriage, is of the reigning king or chief druid joining together with the Goddess to produce a fertile world, or to conjure fertile magick to aid all in times of extreme trouble. The reigning king or chief druid takes on the

the chief druid

a coronet of ivy

physical appearance of the god Actaeon as the Stag King, and during the ritual becomes him. The Stag King will have antlers tied to his head in some fashion, and will be mostly naked in form, except for sacred markings in indigo upon his face and body and leather tied around his hips. The witch chosen to be Goddess for this ritual will be dressed in as much finery as possible, with a transparent or opaline gauze veil over her face and a crown of ivy upon her head.

The secret of this joining is that the actual moment of unity is kept sacred, and both the druid and witch must experience and use the Otherworld power to which they are connecting. If any part of this ritual becomes enmeshed with human lust, then the magick is lost and the ritual will be ineffective. This is a most ancient ritual of immense power, and one that should be revered as most holy between each tribe or between coven members.

The Great Rite is traditionally performed at the sabbats and esbats, but is also performed in times of need or danger when the power generated by the mystical union can then be directed for good. It can be either symbolic or actual, depending on the wishes of the coven members or tribe. Whichever way is chosen, before enacting the Great Rite it must be stressed that this is a holy and devout union, the outcome of which is to raise the primordial magickal force for the benefit of the living worlds. Sex magick is revered as sacred and potent, and should be performed only by those who fully understand its spiritual aims, and between those who know and trust each other implicitly. The magnetic current that is raised between the two persons conducting the rite lets them become repositories of magickal energy, which can then be directed for use.

The ritual surrounding the Great Rite includes feast-making beforehand, used to stir up the elemental forces into the unfolding magnetic current and to set the scene for the later heightened magickal powers to develop. The witch Goddess and the druid Stag King initially sit apart at opposite sides of a clearing but within sight of each other. This is important, because during the course of the feasting and merry-making, a strong flow of magnetic energy will grow and pass between the two, which ignites when they finally come together. The surrounding revelry adds potency to the remarkable and otherworldly link between them.

at the great rite—a feast

The organization of the event can commence anytime from noon on the intended day or sabbat. A wooded or outdoor area is selected, and a large clearing made . This is then ringed by stones or wood pieces, which form the outer boundary. A space is left open at the East point of the ring, which denotes a doorway. The stone or wood that should sit at the East is kept aside for later use. Tables and seating, whether of wood or stone, are set up within the ring, with one small table at the North point of the circle for the witch Goddess and one at the South point of the circle for the druid Stag King. At the West point sits a small altar that can be highly decorated, and upon which sits a chalice of red wine, the witch's athame, and a red candle. Ribbons, roses, ivy, holly, and mistletoe are relevant decorations. If you have the means, a spit-roasting duck or goose adds a nice touch. In any event, there should be a bonfire of sorts within the circle, whether you use it for cooking or not.

Food and drink should be of the witches' choosing. Suitable drinks are water, beer, ale, barley wine, red wine, mead, cider, and elderflower champagne. Food could include chicken, goose, duck, pork, bread, potatoes, lentils, onions, leeks, pumpkins, rutabagas, oysters, salmon, fresh herbs, eggs, dates, apples, peaches, grapes, strawberries, and prunes.

The ritual

Everyone enters the circle or clearing. The witch chosen as Goddess sits at her table with two attendants, and the druid chosen as Stag King sits at his table with two attendants. The rest of the coven or tribe, including bards and harpers, make merry and feast about them. At midnight exactly, one of the druid's attendants sounds three blasts upon the horn and the other attendant collects the chalice of wine. Both attendants of the witch Goddess go to collect her athame. Now the circle falls silent, and the coven and guests file out through the doorway, leaving the two together, and closing the doorway with the stone or wood put aside for that purpose.

The druid Stag King walks over to the witch Goddess and raises the chalice of wine, saying: "I am the Stag King who roams the earth and am come, Great Goddess, to worship thee with my body and in doing so, set light to the sun god's flame."

The Goddess inclines her head, lifts back her veil, and dips her athame

sacred chalice

into the chalice of wine, saying: "I am the Great Goddess and I know thee. My body is the altar upon which the sun god's flame survives, and in this sanctified union is reflected the blessed union of the two worlds. So mote it be."

At this point the Great Rite may be finished, using only the symbolic union of athame and chalice to denote the magickal union of male and female. The rite would be finished by both of them drinking from the chalice and exchanging one kiss on the mouth. At this point the relevant spellworking would be performed, with the return of the coven members if required.

If, however, sex magick is to be raised, then the rite continues thus: the Goddess then disrobes and is given the chalice to drink from. She hands it back to the Stag King for him to drink from, and they both finish the contents. The druid then gives the five-fold kiss: once on each breast, once on the navel, and once on each thigh. The worship of the body then continues in its own way and in private between the two, culminating in the act of love—the sacred union of male and female polarity that gives rise to extreme magickal forces. The relevant spellworking would then continue from this point.

Spells and Supplies
Spells

Spells sometimes take a little time to work and sometimes work immediately, depending on the ingredients used and the powers invoked. Remember that once a spell has been cast, you should carry on with your life, knowing in your subconscious that an effect is on its way.

Before you begin a spell, read it carefully to familiarize yourself with the objects you will need to perform its magick.

i. To banish bad luck

Garlic cloves are well known for their extremely magnetic and absorbing powers, and when negative power is expected, can be placed around the home, or in a witch's pocket. Once used, the garlic must be thrown back to the elements, preferably in water. Be aware that we can create our own bad luck by simply holding onto it when it crosses our paths, instead of letting it flow past.

the garlic clove— most potent magick

To banish bad luck, take a white silk square and draw a pentacle on it with your name in the middle. Light a red candle and place a cauldron of water nearby. Stand with your bare feet on the silk square and hold the garlic up to the third eye (between the eyebrows). Raise your other hand high in the air and invoke the power by saying:

"By sacred power of three times three
Bad luck will fall away from me,
Into the clove, then into the water
Negativity cease from every quarter.
As I will, so mote it be, Goddess bless this spell with me."

Now mentally draw all the bad luck surrounding you into the garlic. Take up the silk square and use it to wrap the garlic tightly into a ball. Then, with all your strength, hurl the ball into the cauldron, shrieking as loud as you can:

"BAD LUCK, ONCE CALLED, BEGONE!"

Now take the candle and extinguish it in the cauldron, again shrieking as loud as you can:

"BAD LUCK, TWICE CALLED, BEGONE!"

Now take the cauldron and its contents outside and hurl them onto the ground, shrieking once again:

"BAD LUCK, THRICE CALLED, BEGONE!"

The spell is done. Take a deep breath and know that good luck is on its way to you.

ii. For good luck in a new home

The best time to move to a new home is during the new moon. To bring good luck into your new home, take a lump of coal and a pinch of salt. Stand facing outward at the front door, and throw both the coal and the salt over your left shoulder into the interior of your new home, saying:

> "Salt and coal in the kitchen,
> Love and truth in the home,
> In this house that we now live
> Let joy and harmony roam."

Leave the salt and coal on the floor where they lie, either until the moon starts to wax or until the next time you do the housework.

iii. To protect a new home

To protect your new home from negative forces, sprinkle the contents of five cups of ale around the outside perimeters of your house during a new moon, and keep a pot of daffodil bulbs on your front doorstep.

iv. To protect against being struck by lightning

Take either an oak leaf, a piece of elder or hawthorn bark, or a piece of fern. Draw three zigzag lines on the leaf or bark (or just use the fern as it is, because of its jagged edge), then bury the item six paces due South from your front door. As you bury it, whisper these words:

> "Hawthorn or oak leaf,
> Elder tree or fern,
> Attract to you lightning
> Away from me burn."

V. To protect against colds and influenza

On the first of seven days, make a tea of thyme, honey, and boiling water, then drink one tablespoon of the liquid three times a day on that day and on the following six days. On the second of the seven days, place dried lavender in your shoes and wear for the following five days. On the third of seven days, grate a whole clove of garlic into a square of white cheesecloth, then tie it up into a bag and wear it around your neck for the following four days. On the last of the seven days, recite this charm at noon:

*"Thyme and honey tea,
Lavender in my shoe,
Draw strength to me
And repel illness too."*

vi. To protect against the accumulation of wrinkles

Gently stew a cauldron of peeled and
cored cooking apples, then add five fresh strawberries and
mix with a little water into a soft paste. Store somewhere
dark and cool such as the pantry. In the early morning, for
nine days in a row, go out and collect exactly nine drops of
fresh morning dew and add them to the paste. Immediately
after mixing in the dew on the ninth day, divide the paste
into nine cups or bowls. Apply a portion of the paste as a
face cream each day for nine days in a row. Leave on for
20 minutes. (If possible, use a fresh sprig of rosemary to
apply the paste to the face—use only the fresh herb, as the
leaves harden to pins after a while.) Wash off with warm
water mixed with a little lemon juice. You should soon see a
pleasing result.

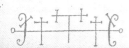

vii. Binding prayer
Draw a pentacle or pentagram image about your person while saying the binding prayer:

"By the sacred name of Sige, she who is above all and every other name, and with the power of the goddess Triformis reflected in me, I exorcise all Ignis Fatuus and I place upon them the sacred sigil of the Pentacle, that they may be bound forever, as with ropes and chains. I cast this evil into the Outerworld, bound forever, that it may never again touch this daughter of the Goddess. So mote it be. Amen."

viii. To break a hex or a spell
If you know what or who it is you are trying to stop, make a poppet in that image as well as possible. Alternatively, make a doll out of plain white cotton, sewn with white thread. In either case, stuff the poppet with thistle leaves and a piece of mistletoe, if you can get it.

Stick the head of the thistle to the
head of the poppet. Now shake a
good amount of red pepper over the
poppet and say:

"Blessed thistle, friend to me,
break this hex for all to see.
    Mistletoe and pepper red,
return the hex to its own stead.
    Blessed thistle, blessed be,
break this hex for all to see.
Amen."

ix. To repel a noisy neighbor

When the moon is waning, sit at a table and lay out these
ingredients in the following order:

Opposite you:	bay leaf and lavender oil
Directly in front of you:	a black candle
To the right:	a stick of sandalwood incense
To the left:	a small glass of water
In the middle:	a mug with a small amount of vinegar in it

Light the candle and incense. Write on the bay leaf your neighbor's name, birth date, and address. Pass the bay leaf through the incense smoke, then burn it in the candle flame and drop the burning leaf into the vinegar, saying:

"Begone, begone, begone."

Now put three drops of lavender oil into the glass of water, saying: "Purify, purify, purify." Then pour the lavender water into the mug of vinegar. While the incense burns down, imagine your noisy neighbor becoming quieter or leaving the area. When ready, making sure you're not seen, take the mug and spill the contents of it in front of your neighbor's house, saying: "As I will, so mote it be, noisy one move away from me." Now wait for the magick to work!

x. Love talisman

Place three drops of clove oil onto a fresh pink rosebud and wrap it in an avocado skin, secured with a wooden toothpick or some string. Place it under your bed to attract love.

xi. To dream of your loved one

Using a pin, carefully prick the name of the one you love onto an apple. If you don't know the name, then prick the word "lover" instead. Place the apple under your pillow. Take a bay leaf and some rosemary and carefully burn them in the flame of a red candle and drop the remains into your cauldron while thinking of the one you love. Go immediately to bed and you should have a visit from your loved one in a dream.

xii. To look lovely

Looking lovely and keeping fit, as most people will agree, can be helped by a good diet with plenty of fresh fruit and vegetables; by drinking lots of water; and by taking up regular, gentle exercise. However, sometimes a spell is just the thing to jump-start your willpower.

Light a white candle and burn lemonbalm oil or incense. Hold a fresh rose in your left hand. Now, concentrating hard, close your eyes and imagine your body taking on a fit and healthy appearance, and your total image becoming more lovely than ever. At the same time, inhale deeply the scent of the rose in your left hand and the lemonbalm surrounding you. Now open your eyes, look into the candle flame and say:

"I am lovely."

Close your eyes and repeat the exercise twice more, then extinguish the candle while saying:

"As I will it, so mote it be."

Whenever you decide that you need to be particularly lovely (for example, when you're undertaking a new exercise regime, diet, haircut, or total change of appearance), make sure that you have some roses nearby and lemonbalm incense or oil burning. If you are trying to avoid overeating, keep the roses and lemonbalm oil in your kitchen near the pantry; if you are intent on improving your appearance, keep the fragrances near your clothes and beauty products—and so on. Each time you need to "boost" your loveliness, you must sniff these fragrances.

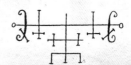

xiii. Money—the tomato

Place a large tomato above or in
your fireplace as a gift to the spirit
world. Leave it there for five days
only, then bury it in your garden.

xiv. Money—the blue iris

Carry the dried petals and root of a blue
iris flower in your purse to increase wealth and fortune.

xv. Money—the candle

Burn a gold-colored candle and hold a silver coin in
front of it until it either sparks and fizzles or burns
down. Place the coin in the softened wax and let cool.
Then put it in a small green bag and carry it around
with you to attract wealth wherever you go.

xvi. Money—poppy seeds

Take the head of a dried poppy and cover it
with gold paint. Let it dry, then carry it with
you in your pocket.

xvii. To View creation

This is a very old spell, known about in esoteric circles and brought to you for the purpose of empowerment. Sige's moment of creation is blazed on the heart of every witch, and central to a witch's existence. Even so, there comes a moment when to see that wonder unfold becomes of monumental importance in a witch's development. This, then, is the spell to create that moment.

Take 20 cups of rainwater and keep it sealed in a glass bowl for 10 days. After that, residue will be seen at the bottom of the glass bowl. Now collect together several candles, a crystal ball, your magick wand, and some consecrated red wine, along with the glass bowl of rainwater. When done, wear a circlet of ivy in your hair and make a circle of candles on the earth in some secret place. Welcome the Lords of the Watchtowers and the power of the Goddess to your circle, holding a crystal ball in your left hand and your magick wand in your right hand, saying:

"Lady Sige, Goddess, the One
Who with command of love, creation begun,
As I spellwork within this hour

Unfold before me sacred power.
As it began, before me unfold
The story of life that every witch
   has been told.
As I will, so mote it be.
Creation with Imperium
   Etherical seal
The secrets of life, twitch now
   and reveal."

Place the wand and crystal to one side to
begin your spellwork. Taking care not to
disturb the residue at the bottom of the
rainwater bowl, pour off the clear liquid
into your cauldron until it is one-third
full. Now set the cauldron in the sun's rays
within the circle.

Take a pinprick of consecrated red wine and let it fall
into the water. At this moment a mistiness and dark
obscurity will develop upon the water. Now let fall two
additional drops, and light will be seen coming from the
dark. Now, acting exactly upon the moment of every
quarter hour of the clock, first put three drops gently into

the water, then four drops gently, then five drops gently, and last, six drops gently, and none thereafter.

With your own eyes, after each drop, you will see one effect after another appearing on top of the water, which are those things that explain to you how the goddess Sige made all of consequence and how creation came to pass. These apparitions will disappear within a half-hour of their beginning, and when they have vanished the moment of magick has gone.

After giving thanks and praise, take leave of the surrounding spirits and close your magick circle, extinguishing the candles and making certain to remove and hide all implements and tools, to keep them safe from prying eyes and purified for future use. Blessed be the witch that experiences this profound spell; it is a great step forward into the light.

xviii. Talisman for a successful court action

Write the name of Imhotep (the Egyptian patron of writers) on a piece of white rice paper in black ink. Draw a red feather (symbol of the Egyptian goddess of justice, Maat) next to it. Underneath these two figures, write your name in green. Tear the rice paper into three pieces. Place one piece in your shoe, bury one piece in your garden, and put the other piece with any papers connected to your court action. As long as you haven't done anything intentionally negative connected to this case, the powers of ancient Egypt should be with you. After a successful court case, take the two pieces of rice paper out to the garden and bury them with the first piece. Make some offering of thanks to the burial, such as wine or chocolate or tobacco.

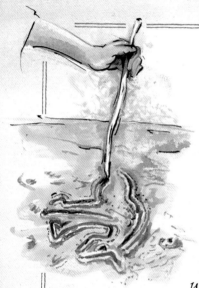

xix. For a safe journey

Take a sharpened willow stick and trace in the earth a picture of the transport that you will be using to make your journey. For example, trace a horse and cart if you are using this mode of transport or a picture of somebody walking if that is how you are going to make your way. Make the picture about 12 inches (30 cm) in length.

Using the stick, go over the image and dig out only the outline of the vehicle. Now fill in the outline with a paste of caraway seeds, ash from your burned incense, holy water (from your altar or a sacred place), and three drops of your saliva. Sit in front of the finished work and trace over the outline nine times with your willow stick, while praying for a happy and safe journey.

xx. For a successful job interview

Write on a piece of paper in this order:

A
BR
ACA
DABRA

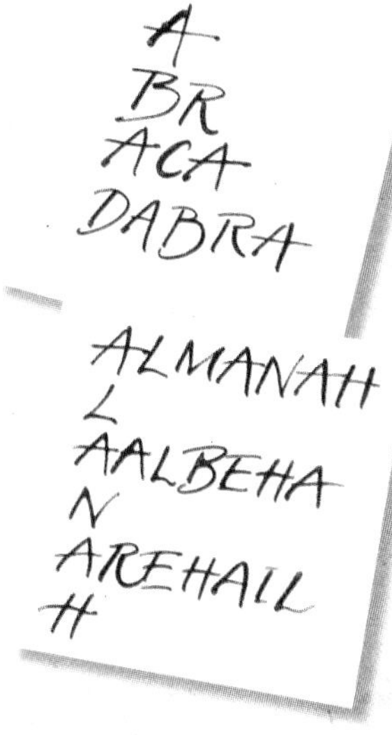

Then on the back of the same piece of
paper, write:

ALMANAH
L
AALBEHA
N
AREHAIL
H

Keep this talisman on you while attending the job
interview, and at any time that you feel the situation is
not going well or to your advantage, secretly touch the
paper and draw strength from its magick power.

Supplies

To carry out spellworking, it is a good idea to gather your own collection of magickal tools. The items listed below are some of the tools most commonly used.

Altar cloth: Designates a sacred space for use when outside or moving about. The altar cloth becomes the altar, and therefore a sacred area, wherever it is laid. It is usually black in color, but is also often red, white, or blue.

Athame: Witch's blunt knife, black-handled, used for ritually cutting doorways, connecting to the earth, and consecrating salt and water.

Broomstick: Used for sweeping away negativity, flying, and spellworking. Often made of an oak, willow, or ash pole bound with dried twigs from broom, rowan, hazel, straw, birch, or willow.

Cakes: Eaten during merrymaking, and during ritual-making with the ethereal family.

Candles: Represent the elemental symbol of Fire. Colors correspond to different magicks. By burning wishes written on paper or leaves, you are sending them through the ether with the power of Fire.

Cauldron: The holy symbol of the Mother. The womb from where all are reborn. The never-diminishing food supply. The nurturing aspect of the Mother Goddess. Feminine imagery— symbol of yoni.

Chalice and water: Represents the elemental symbol of Water. The chalice is used for celebratory drinks, and as a holy water receptacle in rituals.

Corn dolly: A doll-like image made from dried corn sheaves, hung in the house to protect and bring good fortune. It is hung up at the Ostara Esbat and left for one year, then ritually returned to the earth when the new corn dolly takes its place.

Crystals: Used for vibrational magick, communication, and healing.

Goblet and wine: Used for merry-making within the magick circle, and also when drinking during ritual-making with the ethereal family.

Incense: Represents the elemental symbol of Air. Different scents have different effects. Mystic incense is a combination of patchouli, myrrh, cinnamon, musk, frankincense, jasmine, and sandalwood.

Herbs: Used in healing, spell-working, and all types of magick.

Magick wand: Represents Air or Fire. Power in a wand depends on how often it is used, and how it is decorated and revered. It connects you to the ether.

Oils: Used for magick spells and anointing. For a favorite mix for altar oil: Mix olive oil with mint leaves, vervain, marjoram, and thyme; heat gently for a few minutes, then stand for 24 hours. Repeat with new leaves seven times until the oil is a dark, strong-smelling concoction.

Poppet: A doll-like image mirroring someone or something, used in sympathetic magick and spellworking.

Sea salt: Used in spellworking and for purifying; very sacred.

Staff: Two-pronged stick, also known as a stave, used as an outdoor altar and protective magickal device containing spells within.

Stones: Represent the elemental symbol of Earth. Magick stones can be placed on your altar to absorb energy; hag stones with holes can be hung around your neck to trap evil; and sacred and standing stones can be used in rituals and prayers.

White dagger: Witch's blunt knife, white-handled, used in rituals and for cutting and gathering living herbs and plants while outside (ask their permission out loud before you pick them). This is the counterpart to the male athame.

Secrets and Myth

*E*very action has an immediate effect that causes another action. Witches steer clear of causing negativity for a very valid and understandable reason. If you hurt someone deliberately, you are hurting yourself deliberately—and what is worse, you are hurting yourself more than the person at whom you aimed the negativity. The explanation for this is that negativity will always rebound to its sender and increase the sender's own store of negativity. The evil will grow within the sender more than it will hurt the recipient.

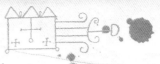

Ethereal Cause and Effect

Once negativity is allowed to grow, so, too, does evil. This continues until the evil content is so large that it destroys itself and its vessel—the sender. Different actions take different amounts of time to wreak their effects, and this is why some people seem to "get away with murder." Any witch will tell you that that person is doomed—for the effect will eventually appear and destroy the cause. Similarly, when one promotes positive production and optimism in all that one does, one cannot help but be rewarded in return with beneficial results.

Rid yourself of blind desire. The more you want and desire a thing without fully thinking it through, the more you will suffer from not having it. The pain of being incapable of achieving your desire is an agony similar to a raging hunger that cannot be assuaged. The more you want an effect without considering the full implications surrounding it, the more your negative energy will grow until you lose sight of the original desire. When you stop desiring a thing or effect, that thing or effect will either come to you and cause fulfillment or you will see that you never really wanted it.

like desire,
the fern
unfurls

By believing in your absolute Will to succeed, you will succeed. This is different from blind desire. The Will to succeed is one of the major secrets of how spells are successfully actioned. It is your Goddess power within and your absolute Goddess Will that make the spell come to life.

Each moment and each spell for that moment has a different and individual time frame. Spells can work immediately or can take months. Never doubt your work once it has been done—this will only cause more delays.

Witches' Lore

*T*he beliefs and ideas that most witches adhere to are listed below:

1. Love and compassion shall be the whole of the Witches' Lore.

2. As it shines above, so is it reflected below.

3. Fir-Fer—Fair Play. As long as you harm none, do what thou wilt—good magick is unending.

4. As I will, so mote it be—the making of magick by the power of the absolute Will to succeed.

at the altar   a spell

5. Act of truth—truth is a vital force. A lie breaks
something; a truth makes something.
6. Fasting—a wrongdoer can be forced to repent by fasting
on bread and water for seven days. If he does not wish to fast,
he must give the accuser an honor price and admit his error.
7. Taboo or Gessa—a forbidden thing. Once pronounced on
a person, a Gessa must never be broken—the loss of honor is
a terrible thing, and the downfall of the person will be
brought about by satire.

8. What use is gold without sun, what use is silver without rain?

9. The power of nine—the magickal time period of nine hours, nine days, or nine years will make a thing come to pass.

10. Preparation, purification, invocation.

11. Consecration, meditation, trance.

12. Incense, dancing, control.

13. The Great Rite—Banais Rigi—Royal Marriage: the Stag King joins with the Goddess to produce living magick.

1	2	3
4	5	6
7	8	9

Akashic Records

*T*he Akashic Records are a collection of moments in time, recorded in the ether and stored there in a vast hall of knowledge. This is a place that witches can go to in order to find out answers to questions, to meet souls from the past, and to learn more about their mystical heritage. All the answers to all the questions are held in the Great Hall of Akash, a wonderful place of true enlightenment.

The Hall of Akash is not the easiest of places to access, but if you truly seek it, you will find it. Many roads lead the way there and some are by way of astral travel, meditation, scrying, and sympathetic magick, but you must ultimately find your own road. What you will learn of there will change your life. If you decide to use your new-found wisdom, be sure that a new book will be opened in the Great Hall and your name will be in it. So think responsibly before you act and be proud of your record in the Great Hall, for who knows who will come afterward and read of your wisdom?

As you explore the marble and stone corridors of the hall, you may notice rooms leading off to other rooms. You may see other travelers exploring. If at any time you feel overwhelmed by the experience, there are guardians and caretakers on hand to show you your path home. These helpers delight in being of use to you, and they will happily point you in directions that may not have occurred to you. Guardians and caretakers of the Akashic Records are poets, and there is nothing they cannot access for you.

The entrance doorway to the hall will change with every witch's viewpoint. Some see it as a large majestic marble slab, others see gold and ebony inlay, and others see a tiny wooden door that could be easily missed in passing. Whatever you see, you must first open the door. Once that has been achieved, then the universe as it was, as it is, and as it will be falls in front of you and is yours to question.

As well as a multitude of books and a vast repository of knowledge, the Hall of Akash has a series of secret rooms that can be used for meditational healing, spellworking, and magick. These rooms are powerful protection areas where no witch is disturbed and where the powers accumulated therein will hold immense magickal properties. In order to get to these rooms, a petition must be made beforehand stating the exact reasons why you need access to such a strongly magickal place. If your petition is granted, you will be informed, and a caretaker will guide you there on your next visit. No witch would ever think of using this special gift for anything other than what it was petitioned for. Although the room itself is secure, once you have left the room, any wrongdoing would be found as clearly as if you were wearing a note around your neck.

At the heart of the Hall of Akash is a temple to the goddess Sige, the Silent One. It is a place that is open and available to everyone. Go there to burn a candle, make a wish, or bring an offering. The Temple of Sige is a holy place with immeasurable magickal power and where miracles occur constantly. Above all else, enjoy the Hall of Akash—it is the witches' special place, where you are surrounded by true friends.

Balance and Duality

The quotation above tells one of the most important cosmic secrets, known since long before the time of the great Egyptian pharaohs and carried forward through the ages under the guise of many secret explanations, reaching a far-ranging school of thought, from the Greek philosophers and the Celts to the East and the New World. This is a power that comes first from Actaeon, the original power of two. It was then brought forth into being by the primal androgyne, anima and animus, and finally into the human realm through the first pair of human twins—Adam and Lillith, Seth and Zoe.

This is the secret power of two cosmic forces which, by their very opposite qualities, produce balance and duality—the Ida and Pingala force emanating from the spinning chakras of every one of us. These two forces have many names and relate to all the opposites in the world, for they are feminine and masculine duality combined. They are positive and negative balance combined.

Together they bring life to all that is good and bad, right and wrong, happy and sad, up and down, hot and cold, in and out, and so on, in perpetuity. In the East they are referred to as yin and yang, and as in all things to do with duality, when they are in balance—when a little right is in the left and a little left is in the right—all is well with the world. As a witch you must strive to keep the balance in all that you do, because that is one of the most effective ways of making your magick strong.

androgyny

The yin element of balance and duality is feminine. She is the death of the Holly King, the anima; she is Lillith and Zoe. Her sacred sigil is an expanding circle that spirals outward from right to left. She is all that is large and soft and ripe. She is the earth in all her fruitfulness and the moon at her fullness.

She is the northern hemisphere in all its cold splendor. Yin is widdershins, counterclockwise. She is peace and rest.

The yang element of balance and duality is masculine. He is the birth of the Oak King, the animus; he is Adam and Seth. His sacred sigil is of a decreasing circle that spirals inward from left to right. He is all that is small and hard and compact. He is the sun in its energy and the stars in their brightness. He is the southern hemisphere in all its hot strength. Yang is deosil, clockwise. He is movement and fight.

When you combine these two powers, you bring to life your spellworkings. The power of yin radiates from the earth in a widdershins spiral, opening up to the skies. The power of yang radiates from the sun in a deosil spiral, compacting downward to meet the yin and be enveloped by her. At this point a magickal energy forms, bringing forth all of nature's forces. You can see this magick moment in every seed that flowers, in every fruit that ripens, and in every child that is born.

The Moon

Selene is the main name for the
Goddess in her moon form. Other
well-known moon goddess names are
Arianrod, Artemis, Astar, Britomartis,
Diana, Hecate, Isis, Juno, Persea,
Titania, and Zirna. The moon is often used in
scrying by catching its reflection in water. The major moons
of the Wiccan way are:

The New Moon: This is the moon's Maid aspect, when it is
initially almost invisible. It is a time for new magicks—for
new beginnings in spellwork—but be aware that it can
produce unexpected results because the moon and the sun are
very close in the heavens. The moon then starts to grow during
the waxing period—a time for increase, luck, and gain in
spellwork. It shows a crescent of light on the right side, which
enlarges until it becomes...

The Full Moon: A completely circular bright disc in the sky,
which brings fullness to all magicks. This is the moon's Mother
aspect. It is the time for fullness and prosperity in spellwork.

> The Witching Hour is at midnight, under a full moon.

The moon then starts to lessen during the waning period—a time for decrease, binding, and protection in spellwork. It shows a dark crescent on the right side, which reduces the remaining light until it becomes...

<u>The Dark Moon</u>: This occurs one day and night before the new moon. The moon shows a light crescent on the left side and is in its Crone aspect, attuned to the spirit world—creating a special time for intense spellwork, such as invisibility and contacting spirits. It then changes to the new moon when the light has disappeared, and begins the cycle again.

<u>The Harvest Moon</u>: The full moon seen in the early evening for several continuing nights in a row. This is because of a varied "retardation" in the times of the rising and setting of the moon, which results in longer light for the farmers to harvest their crops by. It occurs in the months of August and September.

<u>The Red Moon</u>: The moon turns red by reflecting red-colored light, known as earthshine. This usually appears as a

Moonstone and pearl are the gems most favored for moon amulets.

lunar eclipse, and is a portent of great changes ahead. It is a sacred time of power when spellworking is imbued with earthshine.

The Blue Moon: The moon turns blue by reflecting blue-colored light, known as moonshine, and usually appears once every four years, at sacred times of great, powerful magickal ability. Double full moons, also known as blue moons, appear at the beginning and end of a month, and are again due to a time retardation. They usually occur once every 2½ years in months with 31 days. These blue moons never appear in February.

Which day for which spell?

Monday is moon day: good for beauty and fertility spells.

Tuesday is Mars day: good for war and money spells.

Wednesday is Mercury day: good for fortune and business spells.

Thursday is Jupiter day: good for happiness and emotion spells.

Friday is Venus day: good for love and healing spells.

Saturday is Saturn day: good for home and family spells.

Sunday is Sun day: good for peace and mending spells.

The ancient lunar (moon) calendar was governed by 13 months and eventually supplanted by the newer solar (sun) calendar of 12 months. Some countries use a combination of the lunar and solar calendars.

The New Moon is a time for new beginnings in spellwork, but be aware that it can produce unexpected results due to the Moon and Sun being very close. The Waxing Moon is the time for increase, luck, and gain in spellwork. The Full Moon is the time for fullness and prosperity in spellwork. The Waning Moon is the time for decrease, binding, and protection in spellwork. The Dark Moon is a time for intense spellwork, such as invisibility and contacting spirits. The Blue and Red Moons are immensely sacred times of power, when spellworking is imbued with earth and moon shine.

The Winds of Change

There was a time, many, many moons in the past, when the sun fell to the Earth and in doing so became dark and the earth was shrouded in shawls of gray. Fine mists of ash gently fell and covered the world in a seemingly unending display, and witches everywhere understood that this was the touch of Fire from the southern quarter and the touch of Air from the eastern quarter. For here were the Winds of Change at their most awful. And for a long time it seemed as if the sun and the moon had deserted us and we were alone. But witches the world over stood firm and chanted and sang and believed, and time moved and the gray winds left.

Then there was a time of rain, when the world became the sea and the sea became the world and the very ground cracked beneath us, and the Winds of Change howled most horribly. Then we knew the touch of Water from the western quarter and the touch of Earth from the northern quarter, and still the witches of the world stood firm. Again, in time, the rains stopped and the water returned to the sea and all the ground was new again.

The Winds of Change are moments in time when magick is at its most forceful. There are times when the Winds blow such sweet and gentle breath that witches give thanks the world over for these magickal moments.

Swirling silver mists of damp and sweet-smelling orchids fill my mind. My eyes see clearer than ever, every object focused on is shining with otherworldly luminosity, and I feel excitement, like a restless moontide within me. "They are coming," Sige whispers. "The Winds of Change are coming, and soon all things will move and this stultifying moment will blow away and another time will be with us—the Winds of Change wait for no one; they are born on the ethereal tide of movement that passes through us all."

I throw back my head and take a deep life-giving breath of air, the Winds' scent ever more strong, and I will them to bring all their magickal and defining moments around me and envelop me in a whisper of a silken shawl. These are my true friends that help me to move on; the Winds of Change let anyone alter track and begin again.

Now is the time to do that thing, now is the time to move. And I know that anything I touch at this esoteric time will turn to gold. There are no calendar dates for the coming of the Winds—they swirl and flow as they will and cannot be contained. A witch will learn to smell the changes in the air and notice the differences in her surroundings, and for that brief moment she must act if she is to benefit from the extraordinary power that is the Winds of Change. Strong and terrible, soft and sweet; as they change the structure of the ether around us, we can use this time to make dreams come true and unheard of possibilities happen. A very potent time is then, the time of the Winds of Change, for this is Our Time ...